THE ART OF STEALING

AN ANTHOLOGY

MAHESH BALASUBRAMANIAN

Dedicated to

My Parents

Mrs. Meera Balasubramanian

&

Mr. N. Balasubramanian

Contents

Contents

FOREWORD

Dr. Lokendra Singh

ॐ

It is indeed a great pleasure to write a forward for Mahesh Balasubramanian's new book, his second one to be precise. I met Mahesh in October, 2021 at 'The Hitavada's' literary fest and I immediately struck a cordial relation with him and the bromance still continues.

A very pleasant easy-to-go-with personality, Mahesh is a software professional based in Mumbai. Mahesh's early school and college days were spent in Nagpur and he very fondly remembers his NCC days which he considers his golden days- for a reason. Around same time, the right side of his brain got super active and he started writing mainly around his favourite topics- specifically NCC and youth adventure activites in general.

Once he moved to Mumbai to pursue his career and got entangled in the intricately woven tapestry called life, he lost the touch with the writer within. The left side of the brain dominated the narrative all along and thus, the hustle-bustle of life didn't give him much space for creative writing.

And, then came the zero years for the whole world in the form of Covid! That's the time when he reinvented himself as a writer; the golden touch returned! The COVID years indeed enabled the sleeping, writing, singing and music talents of many of us like a Phoenix from the ashes of boredom and killing inactivity. And, this kept most of us sane during that insane slice of time from our lives.

And well, it certainly got us back a gifted writer! Mahesh or Bala as I like calling him, has a style of his own. Humour is subtle but easily palpable in his writings and keeps the reader in a pleasant mood. His choice of topics is also unique. So, obviously, the suave looking man is certainly very active and colourful deep inside.

Mahesh has taste for indi pop, old golden hits and likes reading a lot. He dreams to write his own book of fiction/ non-fictions in the future. Looking at his flair for writing, repertoire of English literary grammar and choice of good but dictionary-not-required words, I am sure he will crash the stands on bookstores. He has my best wishes for the success of this book and hopeful anticipation for the future ones.

Regards,

- Dr. Lokendra Singh

Consultant Neurosurgeon and Director, Central India Institute of Medical Sciences, (CIIMS), Nagpur,

Ex-National President, Neurological Society of India (2019-21),

Maharashtra Hindi Sahitya Academy awardee,

Accomlished Writer and Poet,

Motivational Speaker,

Great Human being.

FOREWORD

Mr. Sandeep Agrawal

ॐ

I got introduced to Mr.Mahesh Balasubramanian through his writings, and articles published in The Hitavada, the leading English newspaper of Central India. Though I have never met Mahesh in person, it has been a valuable and enriching association with this software professional, who was born in my own hometown, Nagpur, and is now based in Mumbai, since more than a decade.

I have read his first book, "Desi Soup-Err–Men", which was a compilation of nine of his best published articles, and is still available on Amazon Kindle.

The perspectives that Mahesh Balasubramanian pours out into his writings not only looks at the world as it is; but also enhances it with freshness. The hard-hitting, yet crisp humour reflects his love for adventure, which was perhaps imbibed during his college days.

Utilising the most of his free time during the recent gloomy pandemic, he has again churned out some lovely articles, which takes readers on a roller-coaster journey, through various twists & turns, and bring out a bright smile on each face, at the end.

It is my proud pleasure to present before you a fragrant bouquet, titled "Art of stealing". I am sure these will be loved equally by all. I wish Mahesh Balasubramanian all the best for this book, and sincerely hope that he achieves success in his profession, as also, well-deserved accolades in the fields of fiction & non-fiction writing.

Best wishes & regards.

- Sandeep Agrawal
Chartered Accountant,
Qualified Acupressure Therapist,
Leading social activist working in areas of promoting cleanliness, beautification and nature conservation,
Regular columnist in "The Hitavada",
Moderator at Orange City Literature Festival 2021

PREFACE

The art of stealing is aimed at looking at life from a lighter perspective. The world still reels from the ill-effects of the CoViD outbreak as also the psychological after effects, which continues to dominate our social lives at large.

Humour has been the casualty; laughter, fun are missing from the public discourse, especially for last few years of the gruelling, punishing pandemic. We need more of that elixir to drink from, to let go of our worry, fear, care & concern. I sincerely hope that this book serves its purpose- in stealing the frown and spreading the cheer.

Laughter as they say, is the best medicine. The articles mostly, are satire and deal with the minute observations and my take thereof from the day-to-day life. I am delighted in being able to express things which readers can closely relate to. In any case, I would love to hear from you on your experience reading this book and connect on a personal basis; hear your viewpoints; receive feedback and suggestions which will help me diversify into topics you would like to read upon in near future.

As a sidenote, I would like to take creative liberty in summarizing my overall experience. There were several lull moments when I did not know which way to go for a start. Having worked in "mission" mode figuring out things, the closest thing that comes to my mind- is the title of an accompanying article - "Operation Bootstrap". Bootstrap, as we know is a small, hard-wired, humble program that spawns an operating system into life. It is those first careful baby steps that even the world's fastest runner must have taken. It is that motivation before the start of play, that a coach uses to charge up the players in the dressing room.

Writing also has been that seed celebrating life, liberating me in the process; helping me explore new frontiers and thereby, form a new connect with many beautiful minds like the people holding this book :-).

Thank you for purchasing this book and considering me worthy of the personal time it will take you reading this book. I can be reached at:

themaverickwriter@rediffmail.com.

Acknowledgements

I would like to thank my family members, friends and well-wishers. It wouldn't have been possible without my parents' blessings' - seeing them smile in appreciating the writeups has been the biggest motivator to write even more, leading me to believe that I have arrived in life. A very special thanks to my wife Poornima who has been an honest critic and thus helping me shape these writeups in terms of what may be acceptable, or may not go the intended way or being unpalatable, etc, as also giving me the required space. Also, thanks galore to my kid Varun- for giving me the needed breaks whenever I wanted to play like a child again.

Thanks to the "The Hitavada" team, esp Mrs. Aasawari Shenolikar, for accepting my writeups over time, which encouraged me to continue writing and leading me to believe in my creative abilities.

Dr. Lokendra Singh - thanks a lot for being generous in your foreword for the book- considering it came at a time when you were being hospitalized for some health issue- it means a lot to me. I am humbled!

Mr. Sandeep Agrawal for coming up with the foreword despite leading such a hectic life. It was amazing, considering that we never met- still you came up with something based on my writings and our limited interactions.

I would also like to thank Notion Press for publishing my manuscript and to provide the support for fine tuning it.

Thanks to the group of creative luminaries where each individual inspires me to think even bigger.

Thank you, my universe!!

DISCLAIMER

Some parts of this book are works of fiction and others are inspired by true events. Names, characters, business, events and incidents are either extention of the author's imagination or used in a fictitious manner. Any resemblance to actual persons, living or dead, or actual events is purely coincidental. No work is intended to demean or defame anyone.

I

Operation Bootstrap

Looking up to the mission that awaited me, I woke up with a firm resolve, in the dead quiet of the night. Today was the day. had not all the time in the world to fix that damn thing – a security hole opening up invitation for vulnerabilities. There was so much at stake- situation being fluid; things moving at rapid pace; that mail from Istanbul; with no trace of where others, who were in the know, were placed, where things stand, etc.

Very soon the day would start, but before it does, I wanted to cover as much ground as possible, to do damage control for the things gone awry. I had to be more organized and assume clandestine approach in closely inspecting the things in order to set them straight. Before others did, I geared up to plan the day; set up plan 'B'; understand the lapses; and prioritizing them before they are plugged. But before doing the critical numbers, needed to tackle another set of numbers- something that would give me a good head start. The bootstrap would set the mood for my day.

Momentarily dismissing the thoughts of failure, I got up to make tea for myself. I would perhaps get a shot in the arm and make sense of the numbers soon, maybe after I get a shot myself! The mission will hold the key to my day going for better or worse! Lest people are caught off-guard, I sneaked out, in a dim lit corner somewhere. To the place where I kept that device. Numbers, numbers, pervasive numbers again! Seems I cannot ever do away with them; not the least for the problem in hand.

Checked the time - so I had exactly 15 minutes left. Taking up a few deep breaths, I stepped slowly inside the small tunnel to start my work. Inside there were several narrow, dim-lit lanes, each having some vaults dotting along. I knew I had to come back and forth to deal with the alleys, turns and pathways again in the labyrinthine tunnel, so in the first pass made the mental map of the lanes, keys, exit route, everything. And also needed to remember the keys I used in the previous turn along the dark lane; and all the other ones preceding it. I prodded myself - heck, I have been adept at these things! So, what if I have not been good with numbers before. With my keen and sharp eyes at work I convinced myself I would soon be at the top of my game; Have been here many times, emerging victorious. Am sure my memory would not fail me. That is what mattered at the moment.

All the while I had been careful. One mismatch and the game would be over, but would only to be known much later, after some more keys falling out of sync being fed. But I would not be knowing it under the garb of false positives and run the risk of being locked inside in the labyrinthine corridors. Though I could retract at any point and the mission would be aborted, I did not see it that way- for I did not want to see it that way. For sure, I could not afford to fail this time hence chose to burn the bridges, so no turning back for me. I risked people disowning me considering the stakes. Trusting on my instincts, as I started tackling the numbers, I felt the rush of adrenalin inside. I looked out for all visual clues that could now sprout from anywhere. Going by my gut instincts, so far, I had been secretly following right track, alternating between different lanes and capturing the key markings I had made in all the earlier passes.

I checked the time again to know I still had 5 minutes to go about ending the mission; good going, with only 10 percent remaining, I patted myself- the cryptic mission is soon going to see light of the day. But yet, I cannot be complacent now, for the last number I would key in would hold the key to my success or failure, a make-or-break situation indeed. Either the last number completes the circuit or leaves it dangling. If that goes wrong, would only have a couple of minutes in my attempt at redemption, to salvage things. Hence, I came around after mentally running the checklist again of all the numbers keyed in so far, I crossed my fingers and keyed in the last number. And just as I did that, exhilaratingly I jumped at thought of yet another code cracked to my repertoire! It could not have been more rewarding, for I could finish that damn mission within time. At that exact moment, the alarm went off, even as made a quick return- safely to where it all started, sitting in my drawing room sofa.

Meanwhile, few emails threw up good vibes - colleagues I was sceptic about, would positively turn up to deliver their share as promised, shortly before proceeding with their festive vacation plans; the client from Istanbul clarified certain things clogging the previous faulty software release; and here I was, taking the lead, planning the required bandwidth and placing people, to face a hectic day of action. I could now figure out the low hanging fruits that we could deliver for the corrective software release- and hopefully make client happy. All thanks to the morning resolve to make things better; to put things in right perspective; to rightfully assign numbers with precise measure, bootstrapping me to a sunny day.

My wife got up, dismissing the alarm she put on snooze earlier. After a while, I got up too, to accompany her for our planned morning walk around neighbourhood park. Before we stepped out, I briefly sneered at the device- my bootstrap routine; the hard-level Sudoku puzzle that now lay sorted on the tea-table. Right numbers at the right places. Mission accomplished.

II

The last man standing

Of late, 8PM is registered as some eventful time for Indians. Once around that time PM Modiji opened his speech, saying *"Bhaiyon aur Behnon"* (Hindi for Brothers & Sisters) and Indians went into tizzy; similar thing happened with Swami Vivekananda's famous "Brothers & Sisters of America" Chicago speech a century earlier which made everyone euphoric. But now, people were reminded more of the stockpile of cash kept in unknown whereabouts of their homes. So, they started playing treasure hunt in reverse.

Incidentally, I too had to enqueue to make up for someone whom I owed money, but didn't turn up to collect cash I had drawn. I deferred depositing it back, lazily hoping that he would turn up eventually. Instead, we saw news of demonetization that evening. After some dilly dallying, finally the last date to deposit legit cash in banks was upon me, so leaving every other priority behind, now I had to somehow fix the cash somewhere, or run the risk of trashing those. Now, the serpentine queues outside the Banks were a common sight. Other people in the queue, like me, were relatable to the laggard students cramming through the night before, hoping to somehow make it through the year.

Again, it was a dampener to know, that like life's other races, I was late here too, knowing that people queued up at dead of the night, braving the cold and bad breath from fellow account holders. Standing in the queue, you pray for the god at work, the teller, to be as much super productive as a super hero can be. You also pray that people ahead of you just give up *moh-maaya* (worldly trappings) and get out of the way. But alas, they have minds of their own; when they looked back at the "lazy guys", they were emboldened to stay in the game. I just wished there were still another day, yet another chance at making it earlier in the day, at the start of the queue.

But nothing of that sort happened. But something else did; a notorious idea within me soon took shape- to jump the queue and go straight inside on some pretext, akin to a Kamikaze Pilot. So, I headed straight ahead to the bank's entrance, overlooking the raging gaze of some 40 people guessing what I may be up to. It was risky; the anger was palpable and such a mis-adventure had full potential to invite wrath.

"Home loan query", I said confidently, and the security allowed me in. At the counter I whiled away few minutes on home loan I did not need, and in the meanwhile, after getting a sense of overlook by the tellers, I managed to get and fill a deposit slip; got up to leave, but got into next counter instead. I tried maintaining composure though I was little conscious & shaky inside at my only chance of redemption- lest I am shown the door.

Once stamped, I lined up behind in the deposits queue which attracted complaints from people outside, as anticipated. But the security could not prevent me now since I had it stamped- they had to honour my turn. The hue & cry died down and soon my time came. Around same time, the branch downed the shutters, since it was close of working hours. I noticed that it would not have been possible if I were still outside; few guys missed the bus unfortunately, possibly their last one. They now had no option but to keep their cash safe, hoping the deadline would be extended out of the blue. I was relieved, since I got saved of the probable encounter with the hostile depositors on my way out, who saw me jumping the queue.

Looking back, it now sounds selfish what I did at the spur of the moment but sometimes you get carried away by goals. I know for sure, how it feels to be overtaken by someone out of turn. But more than the person who failed to turn up for the money, it was the last person in the queue to whom I owed more. A sincere apology.

III

Editor Paramo Devata

(Editor is the supreme lord)

Talking of articles published in a daily newspaper, which is basically where my creative writing pursuits developed wings- it is a treat reading them and getting a perspective on things small & big. But it is pure ecstasy, when you happen to be that author, and you come around to relish it over a cup of coffee. That goes on to say that you are entitled to have the ego when nobody in the world except your own self counts you as a VIP- at least you are happy in your own company and nothing else matters, provided that now you are not bored in your own company. It provides your mundane life with short bursts of ethereal feeling- you feel intoxicated, witnessing your creation attached to your name in print.

Every dog, I am told, has his day- a middle writer is not an exception. Why a dog for a metaphor, you may ask? Well, to set the stage- though a dog lacks the intellectual depth & philosophical leanings of a writer, it serves a good metaphor for explaining writers' disposition in general. As household pets, we know how useful dogs are for outsourcing some of the non-core activities, like- fending off the cats, barking at the guests, and getting it to fetch our newspapers when requested. Provided, of course, that you are on friendly terms with the supreme canine family member.

But again, not every day is Sunday. You know, you cannot have your way every time with the pen and the lady luck sometimes ignores you for an irritatingly long time to come. Speaking of writing articles, even if you are a regular freelancer, you are, every now and then deprived of that pride of place in the newspaper– there are some obvious reasons here at work: Writers' block; Master's choice (Editor blocks!); or other dogs around the street (sheer competition).

As famous French writer Andre Breton once quoted - "Of all those arts in which the wise excel, Nature's chief masterpiece is writing well". Well, quite inspirational indeed. But often times, the perennial itch to write a masterpiece does not materialize even in the wildest of fancies. They call it a writer's block, when a writer finds own self in vacuum, short of ideas. You may prefer to call it the intellectual constipation; or equate your situation with some rudder-less ship; or better still, for a better, powerful impact- you are comparable to some direction-less, leaderless political party headed southwards.

The numero uno reason for writer's block– lack of an environment conducive of creativity. The list goes long, but it could be your hostile home-mates, whose opinion may differ from yours' as regards the creative contribution you make by way of write ups. Or it could be Chintu, the kid next door cast in the mould of Gengez Khan, who would not compromise from his tradition of screaming aloud in a fit of nonsense- until and unless you too screamed with twice the amount of energy that he took to put a question mark on the very fragile existence of glass windows attached to your home sweet home! Evidently enough, the creative juices give way to aggressive cortisol levels playing pole vault internally in your bloodstream.

The editor too, sometimes holds back the great article you wrote, painstakingly inspired by the revolutionary idea that was revealed to you by the universal forces, at the middle of your bath. Perhaps the idea was not decent enough to be pushed to the print queue. Or maybe it was filled with monotony and lacked shock value. I repeat – perhaps it was filled with monotony and lacked shock value, hence got rejected. I may sound like repeating myself, but that achieves twin purposes- 1) to make a point about redundancy; and 2) to make an important point about pointless writings. Geez.

On a serious note, never let your readers keep guessing about your motive- they have the right to question whether at all you are taking them somewhere or just going to repeat things as if a boring number going forever on loop. Anyways, the honourable editor, in a larger public interest feels that such a bold idea may prove detrimental to the interest that the readers have in the newspaper. So, the editor, instead of putting it in the rickety machine, which was perhaps not oiled for quite some time, throws it away. In plain language, you are not worth the time it takes readers to read your views. Being a good, perseverant dog that you are, you may choose to treat this as an indication to fetch the ball and bring it back to editor in a new, but hopefully acceptable shape and colour at a later date.

Sometimes, the article falls prey to pure competition. Your creation lacks the "punch", and appears "forced", since the creative juices in you are not flowing as much as they should be, which explains why you do not stand a chance vis-a-vis other dogs around the street. As prevention is better than cure, articles are never accumulated to take on the configuration of leaning tower of Pisa on the editor's desk. Again, the editor has the temerity to trash your masterpiece to dustbin, so as to avoid having to face the problem of choice in the future. It is like- now or never, placing you at par with a dog lost in a dogfight.

So, each morning it is again- a long wait for the newspaper guy after the Sun god, to appear on the horizons. At about the same time, labourers putting up in the nearby construction site, pass by urgently through the long road to attend to their morning business. They are visibly as gripped as I' am- though for some different reasons which are biological in nature. Hence, I fix my gaze the other way, having made through yet another article after overcoming my temporary intellectual constipation; so, I rest my case and wait hopefully for the newspaper to make my day.

IV

The art of stealing

Since ages, the kleptomaniacs have been treated harshly, while willful defaulters are having others' cakes and at will eating them too! Well, not anymore! For, this piece may rid the kleptomaniacs of their guilt to some extent. Not without reason, as a child Lord Krishna is often remembered as *Maakhan-Chor-* (the quintessential thief who steals butter) - he innocently got away every time after getting caught. Also, since the time of Radha and Krishna, falling in love is often described beautifully as stealing someone's heart, isn't it? Stealing has been and will remain a glorious tradition of our country. Intriguingly it acquired bad connotations thanks to the so-called intellectuals.

A glaring instance is the music industry. They say the lyrics is dead, and it is not hard to comprehend why it is so. Consider the Rapstar Badshah's *"Ye ladki paagal hai"* number- you'll know what I mean when you try making sense after coming out from half dead state. Same thing with the tunes, which reflect on the saturation point the industry has come down to. Other times, "Inspiration" keeps the industry going. How and where they source their lyrics/ tunes from, is an open secret. They get "inspired" to steal, but their popularity overrides the fact any day. Even if royalty is paid for, any such copyrighted work is a "steal" in the deal, considering the eventual big fortunes made by them, ensuring their booty becomes legal tender! That translates to no stopping for the musicians and lyricists, thanks to institutionalized stealing! Re-packaging/ remixing an art to suit contemporary tastes is also an art after all! It is a win-win situation for all. Old wine, new bottle.

Stealing is considered a virtue- as our tradition goes, barring the Nirav Modis' and Vijay Mallyas' of the world, of course - who subscribe rather to abuse of system. Stealing, whereas, is more about optimum utilization of resources. Consider my case for example. The other day I planted a sapling in front of my house. It required a tree-guard to keep the cattle off and continue growing unhindered. To secure a tree-guard however, was a problem- so I went ahead to a nearby park for that purpose. Finally, my eyes caught one- since the tree inside had outgrown, it really was not needed there anymore. And just as I started working on it, some official taking cognizance of it, halted to inquired about my credentials. He termed what I did as an act of stealing.

Without blinking eyes and stopping the great work, I questioned him about the need for it there, since it already outstayed its purpose. He clarified that public property is not meant to be stolen. Misguided that he was, for it was not stealing, but an act of robbery, as it was done with everybody in full view. "Whom should I meet to seek a permission for that, then?", I asked. He looked here and there and said, "See, you can arrange one from here itself, but it is better to come during night when there is no one in sight". Now that made some sense and sounded poetic too- "night" rhymed well with "sight", so I took his sane advice.

So. Let us inculcate this virtue and remove the stigma associated. A bill can be proposed in the parliament for legalizing the act of stealing. Suitable amendments can be made in the acts of various laws to differentiate between the terms "robbery" and the "stealing". The term should be well defined to prevent its meaning from getting corrupt in due course of time.

An academy be set up for grooming the budding young professionals. Remember that stealing is an art as well as a skill, requiring a rare combination of strategic acumen. Awards may be constituted for the upcoming meritorious professionals. The toppers may be considered for special spying missions, for example- to steal critical info of national interest, and also stealing back the Peacock throne and Kohinoor diamond. And lastly, for those calling our beloved PM a thief, be forewarned. Love it or hate it, article 370 clandestinely got vanished right under watchful eyes, a feat deemed impossible earlier. It is similarly just a matter of time POK is also rightfully wrested back into the political map of India.

As Mahatma Gandhi always felt, one should possess only that much, that one reasonably requires. As a nation, today we require to implement this more than anyone else. But in today's world, ironically, no one seems to follow that voluntarily. Everyone agrees in principle but refuse to implement it willingly in their own lives. Hence, socialism kicks in- the government acts Robinhood, robbing from the rich in form of taxes, for general welfare of the masses. But stealing goes a step further- it removes social inequality. Stealing offers a lot to the society apart from removing unemployment to a large extent. Thieves bring in equality in income distribution and help in bridging the gap between the haves and the have-nots.

V

Of Doctors and the doctored

"An apple a day keeps doctor away"- the old proverb stresses the importance of consuming healthy food items, like apple, in keeping us healthy and keeping the doctor at bay. Well, it is true but on a one-dimensional plane; many have rather become paranoid and despite following all health measures (including healthy diet), frequent the clinics for allaying random fears. At another spectrum (as is the common knowledge) are people who shunned CoViD appropriate behaviour, and still shudder at the thought of seeking medical help for various reasons that are more or less, irrational.

The resistance is understandable in smaller kids, though, due to painful memories associated. As a new-born, it was (as usual) a love-hate kind of relation my kid Varun had with the Paediatrician which continued for some years beyond his diaper age. Being carried in arms, gaze upwards in our visits- it took him first few visits to neurologically establish the fact that the sign-board hanging above the clinic entrance is suggestive of a wailing session awaiting inside. On all subsequent visits we faced the music at the entrance itself, causing sometimes the doctor to allow us in, skipping the queue. Dr. Dandekar has been our lucky Mascot- for using his name was a sure-fire strategy to bring the kid to comply with things, like- finishing food properly, behaving his best, go to sleep in time, etc, lest that danger man in white coat would re-surface! *Lammm..bi khamoshi* (elongated silence) ensues!

But. If there is that one quirky thing about the medicos and you are bang on- the writing is clear on the wall- yes, the writing; their handwriting! It is quite mysterious how the connection between the doctors and their abstract handwriting art came to be, but deep in the psyche, people thought high of them by default; they got assured of best diagnosis/ treatment. In a way, the prescriptions allowed them a good word of mouth publicity.

Back in the childhood days, our family doctor happened to write prescriptions in arty, beautiful way. By yet another co-incidence I never regained health by the first few visits to her clinic. But evade her totally- I could not, as her clinic was a stone's throw away from our abode. Well, am not dropping any hint of animosity here- stone's throw is just a figurative part of the narration. And of course, am not generalizing things here. You would find some exceptionally gifted doctors who are at ease with the scalpel and who also know the pulse in the literary space as well.

I remember my mother's post-operative medical reports long time ago- they were mostly hand-written. Those appeared like a convoluted way of putting the signature in 2x speed, while travelling through beaten road in a state transport bus, many times over, in trying to get it right. Or put it other way, imagine *Diwali* rockets launched horizontally, smaller crackers tugging along.

At the same time, it is a wonder- how all the medical professionals are able to accurately decipher such things written by other doctors. As if behind such reports lie a deep secret codified using a code language. As if the reports were perhaps meant to be "confidential", keeping the patient out of gross details. It is also a wonder though -how the young, unmarried "suitable" medicos, in the pre-email/ texting era, used to express the matters of heart in writing? Perhaps some of these expressions were understood well, resulting in professional marriages.

It is also not surprising to come across a word mis-spelt or two. They can be excused though- after all, they deal so much in those Greek sounding infections/ illnesses and medicines that are at best tongue twisters for us. I recall a doctor I once consulted for some illness. Against his prescription, the druggist gave me a bag-full of pills, which seemed to contain a brand less. On reconciling however, I realized to my horror that the first item (which, like others, sounded medicine to me) was in fact, my father's name naughtily reduced to Bal-rub-seminum.

I had the good privilege of knowing a few doctors. A relative being an ex-Army officer, decorated for pulling off a heroic one in 1971 war. And till the day the renowned cardiac surgeon decided to call it a day, he used to visit some village every week for treating the economically under-privileged without charging them a penny, for he considers serving the poor as a service to God. Similarly, another one who started as a compounder, and egged on by his divine skills, he pursued BAMS to open up clinic. Having grown in stature, his expert diagnosis used to draw patients from far-away places. As is believed, a patient well diagnosed is well-treated half way already.

Doctors, of course, are demi-Gods; And a few wolves in the medical profession who jeopardize the patients' lives for their vested commercial interests cannot change the mass opinion. The scribblings are "signature" style of expressing their angst perhaps- given the disgusting ways of some patients in general, and particularly what we all have collectively witnessed for the 2 dark years of CoViD.

Given the current morass, I guess any disclaimer signed beforehand fails to provide sufficient immunity to the medical community. In the pandemic times, when our collective conscience stood assured by the caring, divine presence of medical professionals- the object of utter disgust was, of course- the filthy politics behind arming ill-informed masses against the well-researched, PPE-kit wearing gods. Arming the masses by propagating ideas, like for example, that the incumbent government is out to sterilize members of certain sections of the society; and other such bullshit.

The visuals are still afresh of the savage stone pelting at medical staff that was out to ensure mass immunity. Those images fail to go away from our memories. If given a choice of switching places, us self-respecting mortals, who take pride in our sense of balance- at their place would perhaps want to shoot down the aggressors, would we not? That is why it is unfathomable switching places with the doctors. It takes guts and higher spiritual strength to rise above petty issues, really, to be of service to others!

CoViD went down the mankind's history as the biggest disrupter ever known. The war then was not just against the disease but also against fallouts of collective depression and misinformation. The medical fraternity as always, did every bit they could, in silently fighting them all. Sadly, as we do to the soldiers during war, people remember the angels only during a health crisis and they are back to their old ways out of habit. It would perhaps be a good idea to turn a new leaf, turn the table, and ask the doctors about their well-being, and ensure so!

Because, unfortunately, every time a doctor/ other medical staff if manhandled, say, in case of any casualty because of an operation gone awry, the society at large pushes the angels further to the wall- where the writing is more profound, and it is not about handwriting, but reading- which the society failed in doing so far. Reading- that, by subscribing to such savage acts, we are only perpetuating the karmic misery; reading, that albeit placed in a spiritually higher pedestal, the medicos are humans after all, putting their best possible efforts to save lives; reading, that the society chooses to look the other way, hence ignoring the prescription that reads: Rx- a chill pill.

VI
Treasuring Childhood

It was a summer afternoon when, I returned home dog tired. After the hectic days' work, it was again the same feeling. The dryness outside, in the atmosphere resonated closely in the dryness inside. Dryness- leading to a desire, which I know deep within, can never be satiated. Desire- to be a child again. But despite the futility, humans play around with the idea all the time.

Having said that, we are children after all, howsoever may we convince ourselves otherwise. We call ourselves mature but in reality, we still act childlike in many situations. We may call ourselves adults, whereas we are grown up children really. We many a times come across people scoffing at us, asking us to grow up, or that we are so, so childlike. The reality is, only our toys change, varying incrementally with age. That is precisely why we "toy" up with different ideas different times, be it in matters like opting for occupation, selection of life partner, owning up a vehicle, house, etc. And we detest sometimes, if things do not go our way as planned, in a stubborn, childlike manner. That explains why everyone want to go to our childhood years; why we think those were the best years, bereft of responsibilities and why, given a break, vacation or a sabbatical, we would like to re-visit and perhaps, live out our lives as seen through the eyes of a child. Few people, generally close acquaintances do notice the child like qualities in you.

But as it always happens, I dismissed the idea as a "childish" one. It is like a never-ending conflict between what we wish and what we get in the bargain. Anyways, I am too exhausted to pay any attention to anything, so I retire to bed.

A familiar voice pushed me off my slumber in the evening. My aunt from Jabalpur came to join us for a short stay. After exchanging pleasantries, she handed me a conch-shell which left me wondering for a moment. Then, after recollection, my face lit up and I smiled in delight. "A gift to you from the past"- she smilingly said, appreciating my memory. The worthless conch-shell my cousin sent for me refreshed my childhood memories. Time to re-live, so went on one of my favorites from Jagjit Singh collection- "*Ye daulat bhi le lo...ye shohrat bhi le lo...*".

It was one of those times when we frequented my cousins' place during the longer summer vacations. One day, we friends' together set out for our day's program. We went uphill to a large hillock near the village, roamed and played games, which ran like "papa goes to the office while mummy feeds the children" with small "give and takes". Throughout, we had bursts of laughter and screams which made no head or tail. Our pet dog Moti added the charm to our "Antartic" expedition. That's when my cousin spotted the shell and kept it with her as a treasure.

Looking downwards to the town engaged in made rat-race, we felt ourselves "above" the worldly affairs. We were certainly richer that day, playing adults but without any serious need to be likewise. Even the god seems to have joined us in our laughter as we whiled away our time from dawn to dusk.

As the Sun started setting down on the western horizons, we decided to return home downhill, only to realize to our shock that we had lost our way. Our fears increased along with the darkness. We were horrified. But somehow, seeking refuge in better sense, after asking for directions from different people, we finally traced our way back and reached our homes safely.

After the holidays were over, it was time for us to return as our respective new school sessions had started. Days, months and years passed and I nearly forgot the treasure we found during our shared childhood. Now, after so many years, the toy, the conch-shell, now a temporary escape from the hustle-bustle of daily life, is back in my hands.

"Woh kaagaz ki kashti, woh baarish ka paani..." and the *Ghazal* came to a halt and so did my journey. Oh no, so that was just a blast from the past? Oh, how I wish it were not! How I wished that God allowed us a chance to revisit the past; I would be happy getting lost with the closest of friends in the same bye 'lanes, laughing at our stupid innocence. But nature by itself demands growth along the fluid timeline of life. Hence, regaining my state, I blinked to find myself again in the midst of the people engrossed in serious business. Yet I had that lovely treasure to remind me of the beautiful days of the childhood. A treasure then, a treasure now.

VII
Zindagi Ek Safari

(Life is a Safari)

Animals, like humans are- well, animals. They are known to adapt well to environs as can be seen from numerous findings and the Big Boss episodes. Recently our family experienced it on a trip to the Gorewada wildlife safaris.

Safaris are good way to teach children the fact that animals are way better off –free to roam about and live life like they want without worrying about too many things- sanitizers & safe distancing, dealing with copyright violations, not breaking the wind at royal protocols, or Harman Baweja making a comeback, etcetera. To start with, the zoo is claimed as India's largest, hosting four safaris as of now; and additions as we're told, are likely to be made in near future. What follows are my opinions based on our tour experience.

Leopard safari comes first. Known for their camouflage skills, it is hard to spot leopards here, especially on sunny days, since their deceptive skin tone gels well with the dry grass. Most importantly, as expected- they run not faster, as if on fire, anymore. It is a wonder how the fastest creatures known to go longer distances for food may actually have adjusted to new environs with nil physical activity, given that humans, on their part, grappled psychologically with WFH for the 2-year period for the same hunger problem. Also, the initial tours must have been baffling for them, especially given the visuals of womenfolk- ganging up at every opportunity, what with necks extended, lips pouted at the slightest selfie invitation, etc, thereby conjuring up the images of Nilgai-like creatures seated inside the tour buses, and by extension- relaying off the illusions of an exotic meal. For the numbers- the zoo hosts some 7 of the kind, 2 males, rest females- so not much running around really for the dudes out to woo the girls!

Next comes the herbivore safari. The large enclosure houses around 14 Nilgais' and Cheetals' together. They are having all the fun, for now they seem relaxed from constant fear of impending predator attacks compared to life back in wilderness. Well behaved beasts, as if a notice is posted outside for reigning in the carnivores: "Animals inside are for display purpose only and not for consumption". There was nothing much about the Sloth bear safari, except that they're (2 of them) cute and most unmindful of the visitors- their antics make for fun watch. They remind you of the chilled, Punjabi Irfan Khan voiceover for the bear in the Hindi dubbed Jungle book.

Then comes the much-awaited, but disappointing Tiger safari, housing a male, and another from Venus. It is a dampener- considering a large area, even factoring in, that tigers lead isolated lives and require large land mass to move about, it is almost impossible to spot a tiger. Those not in the know may still feel that tigers are endangered, and that the numbers at zoo is really an interpolation of the tiger population country wide. Which is really a matter of the past and not true, given the positive indicators from last tiger census (2018). This feat ironically was not achieved earlier- even after tiger was made the national animal (1973) in order to save them from extinction, all thanks to the "paper" tigers at the helm of affairs. Comparatively, things look in better shape, now that a no-nonsense tiger prominently heads the nation (since 2014) and hence provides amenable environs for the likes to multiply. As for Gorewada, perhaps they can help by introducing more tigers, if the existing guys have not yet done the family planning already, just in case.

Coming to our experience, it was just not our day- call it bad timing (afternoon); no sightings except for a sloth bear & few Nilgais'. The wild beasts were enjoying their siesta somewhere else after being fed, and hence, figuratively, we were fed up too. The carnivores' feeding area are far away from the route that safaris' follow. That gives them really no reason to get anywhere near you unless they are force starved, and in you they see their lunch. As for your own hunger pangs, the café of "Vishnu Ji ki Rasoi" caters lip-smacking dishes really well, which was the saving grace of our trip overall.

Secondly you need to be lucky enough to have protocol bound co-travellers who value silence enough, so that the feeble voices can be heard to supplement the first-hand observations made on the fly. Our co-travelling *Nari-Shakti* (empowered-women) brigade made sure to use their lung power to the fullest at slightest visual cues. Hey look-a grasshopper! Due to them, the guide with his hushed, henpecked volume was rather indicative, that the tigress, his better half, was "right" behind him and not "left" behind at home as he believed it to be.

We were told that since almost a year back when the safaris actually started, the inmates' biological clocks seem to have adapted really well to those of the humans. That indeed, is evident, since going by Nagpur Standard Time, their day starts late, if the rare sightings of the royal selves are anything to go by. So, I doubt they will forego their acquired lifestyle anytime in near future. To which I am reminded of an old saying "You may take a Nagpurian out of Nagpur, but you can't take Nagpur out of a Nagpurian". That in short was how our safari got played out.

Disclaimer: The creatures called autorickshaw-guys are almost extinct in that region, so do not expect one to come by for a ride back home. Even if one does, they attack without provocation or remorse- on your wallet.

VIII

The Prem Chopra Effect

Admittedly, the world without multiple HD TV channels were the good old days. We were so sorted back then, since the only choice we had was *Doordarshan*. Entertainment was a concept limited to a Saturday evening Hindi film which mostly used to be some *Parivarik* (defined as Alok Nath, before 8PM IST) drama, featuring a 70s' hero beating the villain to the pulp, with us kids doing the former's bidding. Other days, if you were too optimistic & hoping to catch up with cool stuff, then you were bound to be disappointed.

But the scene is changed now. You have cool stuff being aired all day, including music channels showing a seductress doing pole dancing on a peppy number, while earlier you would land up in *Krishi Darshan* program, witness some farmer called Sakharam Patil, standing on some Agri-farm land holding a big pipe. You may think he would do pole dancing as well. But no. He is there to explain the benefits of drip irrigation.

Decency was the theme that time. But sometimes, some movies came along, which were inversely proportional to idea of studies or sports. To the mathematically handicapped - it simply means that the more meaningful the content, the lesser importance your presence is assumed in the drawing room; and hence the more the urgency displayed by parents, especially Dad, to kick you off from the drawing room.

So, bold movies, like Julie, were seldom shown. Now, imagine a meaningful, steamy scene setting the screen on fire. Now, it is a classified info for kid of your age; hence, at an instant you are asked to go and play some game outdoors. Now, that was quite a revelation to the economists studying the causes of population explosion to realize that rather, some indoor game was contrarily responsible for the population to swell up!

Another reason for this adult exclusivity is, the fear of having to face a barrage of awkward questions from children. For instance, Imagine the meaningful scenes that involved Aruna Irani or Prem Chopra or both – such times, the parents used to remind us of forthcoming exam with an alarming level of urgency, and send us away immediately in another room to study in absolute dedication. This was partly due to fact that TV remote was yet to arrive at the scene in late 80s'. Though you wanted to, you dared not to have a second look at the TV, since your dad's eyes were comparably bigger than Prem Chopras' and emitted equally harmful signals, but with different emotions.

The satellite cable TV was the next big revelation to us in the growing up years. The craze was palpable during the initial years, when affordability was a restrictive factor for some poorer people, for whom cable TV was the iPhone of that time. But there were *Jugaads'* (workarounds), though. Those who could not afford electricity used hooks to hack into transmission lines; while those lacking the network-used their basic DIY multiplexing skills to get seamless viewing experience sans any monthly bill.

The new norm was one TV set per home and that included the remote control. Earlier the TV viewing rights were with the self-appointed-sensor-board guys provided by the mother nature, called parents; but now, slowly the grownups also begun to wrest their rightful claims. Except that now it was no more necessary for parents to remind you about homework every time Mamta Kulkarni suddenly came sizzling on the screen. Just a play of fingers, and the next moment you see Chief Election Commisioner, Mr. T.N. Seshan (without the Mamta Kulkarni dress code), guns all blazing and warning the politicians against doing any kind of naughty activity. He spoke in context of the forthcoming elections, of course, just to clarify (not all politicians are Prem Chopra). But again- needless to say, all hell would break loose, if the remote's batteries go dead during such critical times of meaningful scenes and fail to make the channel switch.

Even the youngsters were adept at using remote control to conform to the Common Minimum Program (CMP) of the family to watch only content that promotes family values and harmony, which also signalled that the era to talk about the birds and the bees had not arrived yet. Anything that is a depart from this CMP, you had to watch it different time, presumably when meaningful content like Baywatch was aired and the parents were practicing *Yoga Nidra* in another room.

Now, cut to the present day & time, we have smaller homes & smaller islands within our homes for each family member. No device restrictions, either. Each one, to his/her own, so they watch meaningful content at their space- whatever may their definition of meaningful be. The result – the rate of generational divide has increased exponentially. The CMP shrunk furthermore- it is rare sight now to see a family having dinner together at a set time, eagerly watching a planned movie on TV. We may be long lost on the legendary movie *Upkaar*, but it serves a good metaphor here. It is high time, we should, at the least, bring the self-centred Prem Chopra character back to drawing room, if not in the farm fields.

IX

Roaches, Roaches...

...everywhere, this is no time to stand and stare". Or better still, the lines doing poetic justice to the eulogy on the cockroaches, if ever written, could go like:
"Cockroach, Cockroach, many in sight, the one on the left, red and bright, is it turning right?".
Irritated am I, you may ask - by the sight of some, or am I being poetic,

Nothing of those, just overwhelmed am I, by the fight pathetic.

Well, Cockroaches have been topmost on my mind these days, after once I woke up at midnight to the sight of large congregation having a ball in the kitchen- near the stove, oven, here, there, everywhere. A clandestine meeting of urban naxals in urban household kitchen. Not the larger of their kind, but the smaller ones- made with German technology, hence named so- the "German" cockroaches. Not that I fear them, but most of us would agree - their disgusting appearance, and the silent health hazard they pose make cockroaches the perfect villains. Despite that, for generations, men used to derive pleasure in the fact that women do fear roaches the most. As the joke goes, men are brave too, until the cockroaches start flying. As per folklore, they are fly to face a certain death, perhaps by inviting the attention of lizards. But again- talking of lizards spotted sometimes in my home, they were driven away on priority, useless as they are, since roaches' figure the least in their elite dietary preferences.

So, it is time for the lone wolf to pick up the arms and wage a war against the pesky pests, am forced to. And the best weapon against them is not a repellent spray- they actually arc meant for you, so that you dare not venture again in the areas you apply them to. So, what's the best option at hand?- Lets park the question aside for a while.

Now as a detour, consider this maths question asked in a competitive exam- on a 25-metre pole installed on the ground, a cockroach starts from the bottom, upwards at a certain constant speed and another one, from the top, going downwards, at 2X the speed. At what place in the pole would the roaches meet? For the mathematically lesser inclined souls like me, the answer would be to pick up a slipper, smash them at their respective places. Which means they will meet never, except in the heavens above. That makes for a one stop solution for both the question (though it is an unlikely option), and the pest problem at hand- slippers make for a great weapon against the roaches.

When it comes to agility, general perception is that the Cheetah makes the cut, but to me, a cockroach wins the race any day. The reason being that we are so familiar with them, and hence, frequently come across them and would rather prefer not to come across a Cheetah in our lifetime. So, let me call upon stage, the winners! Come on roaches, don't fear or try to hide, claim your prize- a pair of slippers!

Anyways. Yes, agility! As per recorded observations, roaches are capable of changing directions 25 times per second on the run!! By that measure, nothing is as quirky a creature as a cockroach. By saying that, I mean to include Srini, my ex-colleague, also in the classification- since he comes close to being a cockroach when it comes to changing decisions. Strikingly, for all the team members, Srini also used to stir same emotions that people (specifically who reject the idea of roaches as a delicacy) personally feel, on being confronted with a cockroach. That is, without making any further movement, look out for a slipper with an eye on the roach.

The most astounding fact about the roaches is that they show cannibalistic tendency in absence of food. A fact claimed to be used well by the pest control. The pesticide kills some, others eat them and are killed in turn, and the chain continues, killing many in a cascaded fashion. So, you may as well imagine how a conversation between two cannibal roaches Tim and Srini may go-

Tim: Nothing to eat today. The house lady is cleanliness freak, must say.

Srini: Yeah, we are helpless too Tim! Hmmm.. Hey, look behind- there comes your wife!

Tim was never heard of subsequently, while Srini as always, appeared well-fed to me.

The nasty pests, am sure are welcome only in the "Oggy and the Cockroaches" cartoons. Except, of course, if your household loves the roach recipes. Now sample a mother in her kitchen asking her kids if they can bring some from the grocery store to make up for the shortfall in preparing the evening snacks - "not needed, Mom- there are a few I spotted in my bedroom, will bring them!". Readers may pardon me for that crude reference, but jokes aside, initially I was in disbelief too. Until someone sent me a video on roach farming in China, that took me several days to muster up courage before I finally saw it, and after I removed that video, few more days to get over the weird feeling.

So, what use could the creepy cockroaches be to the mankind? Seems none, except for a few researchers from a university, where they draw inspiration from the roaches to draw upon a prototype for an ultra-lean robot. The robots could assist humans in evacuating people from the rubble after an earthquake, by sneaking deep inside and reporting vital sightings of people trapped. So, they carry some significance- for they can intrude through even the tiniest spaces that seems impenetrable. Scientists need all appreciation, for they could visualize taking roaches as reference, to innovate something, which for us ordinary slipper- wielding, mathematically challenged people, was unthinkable.

The scientific breakthrough may happen for the useful robots to come up some day, but for dealing with the entomological creatures, it is better to stick - to the slipper or a broomstick. So, after several nights of battling the army of roaches at the stroke of midnight hour, I thought I had won the freedom, but alas, far from it; for I noticed many more sooner, signalling that the battle is far from over. Briefly before the Hitler in me took over, the exasperated Ghalib in me exclaimed:

Wo aaye hamare ghar, khuda ki kudrat hai, kabhi hum unko, to kabhi apne ghar ko dekhte hain.

X

The Dear Departed

"Each day is a brand-new day for the rest of your life"- This symbolizes living life to the fullest. That death is an inseparable part of the life is a universal truth. Though it does bring about morose and vacuum in the lives of near and dear ones, since the loss can never be quantified- it is unfair to let go of precious moments that life has to offer. It is unfair after a certain time to let a death in family cause so much emotional suffering so as to cast a dark spell even over the positive developments that are waiting in the wings. In absence of conscious efforts to overcome it, life is reduced to an exercise of rituals, like a big burden we carry all along our journey to our destination. Hence, after the initial period of bereavement, excessive brooding should be avoided. This is because life is a continuous, fluid timeline, of which growth is an important part and parcel.

Of course, death does bring about change in order of the day. There is a family I know about from a distant past. The elder boy of the family was marriageable age when he died, leaving the parents and the younger brother behind.

He used to outdo his younger brother be it in matters of catching the school bus or making friends and social contacts. This time too, he continued with the same spirit and outdid everyone when it came to embracing the death. Out with some friends on Diwali eve, after a while one of his friends called over the phone to call them over to a particular hospital, for he had collapsed during the *Sai aarti*. The first sight of him witnessed by his family members was of his eyes staring into infinity- for the doctors declared him brought dead. Diwali, ever year thenceforth, alongside the happy moments does bring about those memories for the family at times.

After his death, his brother donned the mantle of "second in command"- the very moment realization dawned on them- as if he could see it coming. It is remarkable to know how sense of responsibility comes automatically to some people, like his younger brother who had so far enjoyed the carefree life of a younger brother. Some things still evoke in him the thoughts of his elder brother, like for example, a song from *Jo Jeeta Wohi Sikandar*, "*rooth ke humse kabhi, jab chale jaoge tum*". He now knew that he had to hold his tears back in order to control that for those around him, especially his mother.

Reminiscing the times, I know the only time he cried was during the final farewell, realizing well, that his big bro-cum-friend, and his partner in crime is no longer alive. He never left his mother alone, tried to bring life back to normalcy for his mother, but in vain. Though a strong-willed lady herself, she now used to brood over frequently. And the root of this was the framed photograph of her departed elder son, hanging on the wall. She would frequent that wall and stare at the frame as if in eternity. That exercise, almost a ritual for several minutes in a day, was causing the glum atmosphere.

To seek an end to this, he removed it & kept it at a place unknown to his mother, on the pretext that it would not bring peace to his soul if she were to stare & glum-laden, remember him for a longer period. Though this change got her unsettled, after initial resistance, she got used to this change in a matter of days, coupled with other "cosmetic" changes around home. The trick did the work.

Time heals all wounds. Thenceforth, and till date, she is a happy-go-getter person that we knew about. Her husband retired some years later and enjoying the peaceful, retired life. The son freely went about his career pursuits, assured due to father's presence at home. On Mothers' Day, I called to wish her and what caught my attention was her WhatsApp profile carrying my snap from the good old times. Happiness is infectious. Happy I am, because she is.

Miss You Bro

XI
The Cyclic phenomenon

The pandemic altered our perspectives like it never did before, and many of us took to healthier lifestyle for good. One such regular sight is people cycling around neighborhood for fun. It caught my fancy too and so one fine day, I had mine overhauled, as it was dusty and needed repair. To be doing something that was part of my much younger self, it was an exercise in recollection.

During my college days, an exclusive moped delighted me. But I was supposed to use the old-fashioned bicycle we already had. A bicycle was a common feature in the middle–class scheme of things. My father used to reminisce how the old bicycle stood like a good companion in his life. A common theme is that luxuries spoil us and deprive us of our share of struggle so necessary for success. I desisted the cycle; it was a vintage, "fitter for museum" no less. But the times were still quite different from today's "use and throw", glut economy. So, a new moped was out of question for me.

"Robinhood" is today the most unheard of a bicycle brand. It was amazing to hear stories around cycling in general, in older generation. That it was a luxury to own a bicycle and that it, at one time, required cyclists to carry "*Billa*" (licence), which was nothing more than a metal plate with a number embossed; how people used to resist having to pay dearly for it; and taking alternate routes on knowing from the passersby about some cop lurking around the corner to catch violators, etc. The most hilarious was a mention about once upon a time- when let alone street-lights, streets themselves were missing from the narratives of our urban lifestyle- that it even required one to carry a kerosene lamp and matchbox while riding at night and stop many times over to alight it if in case the flame went off due to winds.

The cycle had been instrumental behind many a thing: helping Father with the balancing act between his career and academics; brothers' many a win at the cycle races held in the locality sports meets; and carrying me through a backbreaking NCC cycle expedition, the old cycle had been through all. When my elder brother used to teach me to ride, I had this constant dream of someday being tall enough, to be able to "be seated high" & ride through the lanes of my locality. Also, that once enroute to my school, I (ahem) fell into big pit while trying to impress someone with my stunts- but depressed I got instead; causing me to retrace the steps and take leave instead for the day.

It was common for people that time to preserve things religiously, to be passed over to the next generation. And so, many guarded against selling them off. But the old mate had served its time and a new one was to accompany it soon. Incidentally, a popular advert titled "zero-effort biking" was doing rounds. It appealed to me even more since the captain cool of Indian cricket that time, Ajay Jadeja was promoting it.

It delights me to see the cycle repeating with my kid paddling through my locality on a yet newer bicycle, doing stunts, as much as I ruminate on humble beginning of the older one. It takes all types to make the world and my inventory then was no exception. Perhaps, like a workaround for bridging the generation gap, my inventory, then was the intersection of two technologies, or to say two generations.

XII

Diary of an insomniac

It is past midnight, and I am reporting from the trenches of despair, and helplessness. Like the famous "India's tryst with destiny", at the stroke of the midnight hour, I too woke up - albeit to a noisy bladder, thanks to the prodding by a couple of mosquitoes. I know this to be a night longer than usual again. Once the sleep is out of the window, a question comes to the mind- "I am free to do what?". Like an unemployed person free to explore the opportunities, I need to sneak out of room & by shutting the door behind, I ensure I do not become a headache to the fortunate others enjoying sound sleep.

If a book were to be written on the unsteady life of an insomniac, an apt title would perhaps be "A Day in the life of an insomniac". Or maybe night. Whatever; it ceases to matter once the new day arrives and people wish you a good morning. You wonder how to pretend to be happy, instead of boring yourself to death on prospect of being caught off guard at numerous meetings. Surely, you cannot work up enough energy to achieve much work-wise that workday, unless you have those 40 winks. And unless you do, meetings abound will sound so gibberish, so Yash Chopra-*ish*.

Clearly, my circadian rhythm had gone southwards. In the early youth one can go without sleep for 4 to 5 days at a stretch and still not have any health issue, but this was unthinkable for me now. The sounds, lights and hustle bustle of the day had its toll on me. For a lasting solution I am contemplating lifestyle changes and some winding up ritual before retiring for the bed, but for the issue at hand, I sought means to kill the time.

With sleep growing brittle by the day for others too, my household now prefers pin-drop silence at this time of night, so it is a sin to even doing tic-tac-toe with the electric switches. Or anything that has evolved to be able to produce sound. Me, for example, when am in deep sleep (once in a blue moon, of course)- in which case my wife turns insomniac, thanks to the Dolby stereo quality sound from my snores. Other times we stand witness to the democratic voices that transpires in mid-night meetings of the canine community in our complex. To while away time, I check WhatsApp in the hope of catching some like-minded soul of an owl, who may be up at this odd hour. But I end up doing a post-master's job, forwarding messages from one group to another.

After some time, when there is nothing better to do, I decide to clandestinely do the TV on mute. Only to know that there are dedicated souls like me on news channels who lost sleep over the fact that the world cannot wait another day to witness the news breaking. That a cop-turned-convict was made to walk 7-8 times to recreate the crime scene. It is a nice idea to step out for an early morning walk, so taking a cue, I head out.

Once out of home, under the rule of darkness, the *Tezaab* number "*So gaya ye jahaan*" was ringing in my head. But it was loud enough in my head to disrupt the eerie silence for some nocturnal creatures. To them, I was the ISI trained terrorist out there to disrupt their peaceful co-existence. So, the canines, who had other thoughts, reciprocated in the ways they know best. Perhaps its little too early to call it morning, hence they are not too intent to wish me a good one. A little deliberation later, I give them a walkover & stealthily retrace the steps to my home.

XIII

The Left Vs Right Conundrum

Of late, the prime-time political debates make for an interesting watch, for they are as real as the reality shows can get! As such, we consume news debates more than we do soap operas. Packing in the entertainment quotient, they provide respite to your sombre, humdrum existence.

The debates all follow a typical pattern- it starts with stage setting, putting the topic in context, after which one of the sides is asked to put their opinion. Once the ball rolls into motion, there is no need any more for the host to chip in other than to act as moderator & synchronize the turns participants take, depending on which panellist is more qualified to be pitched against the other and answer the point raised. The debate soon assumes high octane volume that once used to be associated with the formula 1 races- which is no more heard of, since the king of good times "left" India running against his time.

The debate is now free for all (a.k.a *macchi market*), and there is no limit to the combined volume of the participants unless the host happens to be Arnab Goswami, the one who is reportedly heard even in the neighbouring planets. You also raise the television volume in the hope of catching up the feeble voices drowned by the aggressive overtones. The net effect is that you are issued an even bigger warning from another room that unless corrective action is taken, you will be assertively treated with iron hands left, right and centre.

My kid, once trying to comprehend a political debate too complex for his age, posed me a few questions, like- who is talking sense- the one on right or the left one? And what is meant by "left/right political thoughts", etc. While trying not to be judgemental, I tried to cut through the complexity with some reasoning and little success. Though examples abound of polar opposites in the universe, like right and wrong; Mars and Venus; sanity and Navjyot Sidhu, etc, the difference about left and right political school of thoughts, I realized, is not just a linear, binary difference, it is much deeper.

The new political order places all the parties which go against the establishment as the "new" left. A curious case is a grand old party devoid of any introspection- it no longer requires any palmist of repute to reveal- as to why, like its political heir-apparent, the party's fortunes are headed southwards. Not many are "left" to stand with them in the political scene. Officially, they don't claim to be left leaning, but politically speaking, that is like saying Fardeen Khan is different from Arjun Rampal, in terms of acting prowess.

Now, call it superstition, or by plain design- the "new" leftists, given the honours, seldom start the debate on right footing. The debates are witness to this and they open up a world of hypocrisy that audience, the electorate has been enduring all along. The sane minded viewers are jinxed - they wonder as to why these ill-informed people should, who are far removed from the ground realities are called to the debate at all; or they start doubting that too much of democracy has led us to this state- and that these people would be better off damned to see all the Arjun Rampal movies. In one go.

And it so happens that most of this noise is contributed by the new leftists- the different spokespersons represent their exclusive top brass gone into recluse after tweeting something controversial yet again and leaving the motor-mouths to defend for themselves. Mostly, leftists are seated at the right side of the screen; why right, you may ask? And you are not alone in this confusion- in a movie, Sunil Shetty's character also wondered- "*Aapka left ya mera left*" (your left or mine?). Well, the leftists, according to leftists, are leftists in their own right, so it's their perspective.

Again, being seated right definitely does not imply being right on moral discourse of providing the checks and balances to democracy. The power tussle spills over to the intensity of the debates too, rendering them inconclusive most of the times. The new leftists, by design have been beating around the bush, whether in debates or in their only-God-knows what ideology.

Here, a point to note is that two wrongs don't make a right, but three lefts do! This is because, technically if you go straight, then make three left turns you will have made a right turn. But as common-sense dictates- apply a right turn, right away, rather than go straight then take three lefts; thereby saving time and petrol.

A logical conclusion to draw here is that the leftists are better left to their fate. The debates on issues tend to be never ending, hence by extension, there's no logical closure expected for the left vs right conundrum.

As for the kid, he would learn to discern for himself in due course of time, until he comes of age, ready to cast his first vote. For all we care to know, the nation is indeed, currently headed in the "right" direction, and geo-politically speaking, the future belongs "right"-fully to India. So- *Yehi hai right choice baby.*

XIV

Don't snore, oh you bore

The other day I decided to pull out all stops and take efforts to bring it to an end and turn things around. My family, especially my wife & kid had had enough. It either keeps them awake all night, or other times am awake myself since they volunteer to wake me up many times over during the night and tell me the truth. In the latter case, it so happens the next day, that I let my expressive, Nana Patekar like blood-shot eyes do the talking. In the office meetings, my eyes are raging enough to nip in the bud, questions like- why am not talking much. So, they know that if I do, it may as well be the last word. Jokes aside, my snoring problem was taking a collective toll on everyone around me.

So, at first, I was aghast on learning that I snore very badly. As a child, I used to wonder with disgust how some elders used to belch out sounds in deep slumber. And sometimes it was not one, but multiple JCB machines at work. But now it was time to accept the truth that I had crossed over to the other side of the table, too. And one fine evening they helped me with the transition and getting past denial mode by recording my snores to be later played out to me. Evidently it was a dark spot for me and hence I was in denial mode for long till I realized I was at risk of being equated with the grand old political party of India, which similarly, had denied any connection between misgovernance and poverty, which explains why they no longer use the (I) suffix where the I stands for the missing Introspection. They have become their namesake, a good for nothing shrub.

The tipping point was when I was forcefully woken up to be told, "Mahesh, Oh Mahesh- Oh, such a loud snore! *Tum jaakar so jao kahin aur.*" (go sleep somewhere else, you loudspeaker). Which means it was high time to do something about it lest I be transformed from being a better half to worst.

It typically poses embarrassment, especially when we expect guests staying for couple of days with us or when you are travelling with the railways on an overnight journey. It is one thing to be cordially greeted by your fellow passengers the evening before, and another thing to be snubbed; you can subtly notice the change in co-travellers' stance, they were friendly last evening but chose to look the other way next morning. And you know the reason. And you know well they would not continue with the policy of offering you something to eat for the rest of the journey. Which in short means *Katti* (cutting off friendly ties). Once my vocal fellow travellers even told me that the previous night, they could not hear out each other properly, thanks to the Dolby stereo speakers that comes alive once am asleep.

The snores had reached huge enough proportions to be mathematically defined as Mamtaa Banerjee squared. I tried laughing it away by stating that the married men seldom get to speak when they are awake, so the snores are just a gibberish manifestation of the suppressed expression of opinions. That did not help in any way the cause of oppressed husbands, though.

People with some experience struggling with snores will relate how futile the entire exercise is. My experience with nasal strips has convinced me as well, that there is only one-time solution to snoring problem – the nose is plugged with cotton, a quintessential Hindu ritual during the final sojourn. That essentially means I have laid to rest my desperation for solution, and that we had fresh perspective to look at it as some issue on which I did not have any direct bearing. It was good to have family by your side since they are convinced and acknowledged the fact that it really is an involuntary act by the muscles in respiratory tract and that being obese, or overweight was the root cause contributing to its' amplification. And it is an open secret that weight management is as easy as expecting a tiger to change its stripes or expecting an iota of honest governance from the any ruling dispensation in Pakistan, that instead chooses to look other way.

XV
Ramayana- the modern take

Ramayana, through the ages has been told and re-told by many great sages, like Valmiki, Tulsidas, Kamban, and so on. May I, too, have the privilege of enlightening you with the times of the modern-day Ram-Rajya. So, cut to the times of Ram Singh and the cutthroat world of IT industry. Ram Singh, a top-notch Software professional, was in exile. The exile was forced upon him as one close confidante of the company's chairman, Kaikeyi, shockingly acted on a well thought out plan to bring in her son Bharat Singh to take the position that Ram rightly deserved and going by popular opinion, was pipped to occupy.

After being fired, our hero Ram Singh had set out on a unique path less taken – to create a success story through his own start-up. Though he knew it won't be a cake walk, the overall environs encouraged entrepreneurs and many had quickly matured into unicorns. So, armed with conviction, he decided to give the idea of his dreams a shot. He was not sure how long he would be in exile as opposed to his Satyug counterpart who had surety to return after 14 long years. His unemployed brother Lachchman Prasad accompanied him. And so did Seeta Rao, his team-mate and a promising developer who thought high of Ram. She had learnt a lot under his mentorship, and believed that rooted in principles, Ram could help change the scenario of the software industry. Hence, she was more than willing to follow him wherever he went. The recession was not over yet.

While in exile, the sphere of positive influence exerted by the team of three was not lost on anyone; even the chai-wallah outside Ram's startup, Jatayu was all in praise for them. Jatayu was an ex-software engineer with his wings of ambition clipped by industry politics. The trio was established in "*sarve bhavantu sukhinah*" (may all be in peace, devoid of trouble or illness) or, "*sabka saath, sabka vikaas*" in short. Now, one Mr. Ravan – CEO of another company, who was infamous for throwing his weight around with his strong-arm tactics, corrupt trade practices, and carried a long-standing disrepute of spreading ransomware, chanced to know of Seeta Rao's talents.

So, when our hero was away to find projects, Ravan, using his key HR guy, lured Seeta away by promising her a decent lifestyle working on data science projects. Everyone has a price tag; the HR guy would go to any extent donning role of friend, philosopher, guide, etc, in order to recruit a good Software resource that is hard to come by in Kalyug. Now, overwhelmed by the 200% salary hike and decent early joining bonus, Seeta couldn't resist the offer. Ravan had evil designs of becoming "teeno lokon ka swami" by establishing his monopoly. Jatayu knew Ravan closely enough, and was witness to the proceedings, but was helpless. Ram, on return was told by Jatayu of recent development.

"Ravan, you Rascal", roared Ram. So together went Ram and Lachchman in search of Seeta. On their way they befriended Sugreev, who had faced similar issue that Ram was facing. But thanks to Ram's goodwill and consultancy, Sugreev could get back his partner on board. Hanuman Singh, the 'H' in Sugreev's HR team, was called upon to locate, and roll out a counter offer to Seeta, and thereby do Sugreev's bidding. Ram wrote a letter and handed that along with Java logo over to Hanuman. Seeta, once located, would recognize them and may re-consider returning to Ram's start-up. Hanuman went ahead and tried boarding Mumbai local that would help him land in Ravan's territory. But he was not successful as he was pushed off from the jam-packed train to a SOBO suburb. So, he ventured on his car, navigating through the ocean of vehicles on the never-ending Mumbai roads.

Meanwhile, at his startup, Ram decided to work on vaccines that would counter Ravan's ransomwares and viruses. In anticipation of some good news, he waited eagerly for some communication about Hanuman's return.

Seeta was eventually found, loitering around in Ravan's campus, by now being aware of Ravan's HR bluff. She deeply felt guilty of being the cause of the untoward effects of quitting Ram's firm without serving any notice period. When Hanuman met and apprised her of Ram's counter offer, she was in great dilemma- but chose to rather wait-n-watch. But deep within, she knew it fully well that she can't pull on very long without the required energies with her new job.

On Hanuman's return and knowing of Seeta's whereabouts, Ram decided to meet her personally and convey to her of his vaccine's superiority over Ravan's viruses. Things are finally being turned around. His genius dealt a final blow to the foundations of Ravan's business, which in turn fell like a pack of cards in no time. The old flame now got re-kindled; Seeta obliged to return-impressed as she ever was, by Ram's ingenuity.

The "*Achche din*" are back. On returning to normalcy, Ram Singh, now a formidable name in the industry, attracted offers of joint ventures from all sections of the industry. The recession is over, gleefully he thought. He, however, held his horses back. And eventually came about an offer he couldn't resist either. To his joy, the CEO from his earlier company, sought meeting with him over proposal of a possible merger.

So returned our confident hero on his own terms, happily back into the folds of the company, which he anyways considered his *mai-baap*. With changed order of the day, he had more say in the management and day to day affairs of the company. Thus, went about Ram Singh, on his way to establishing his reign, rooted in principles of fair governance.

XVI

Yours, friendly

Sometimes, the hectic lives that we lead, barely gives us any time to even catch up with our own thoughts. But not so very often, and quite overwhelmingly, there comes a moment when you cannot help but get lost in your thoughts; all you need such times is to be left alone with your thoughts, in solitude. It was one such moment, when the other day, I woke up to find it was my dearest friend's birthday. I looked out from the window and the past sped in front of me.

It was turn of the new millennium, predating the facebook and smartphones. Avi and me became thick friends at a computer institute of yet another good friend, where we had liberty to use the great resources at length. We shared a common fate since we did not own a computer ourselves. So, we spent longer hours with computers, books, and discussions at the institute. Evening times for respite, we frequented the nearby internet café for surfing some websites going through funny emails, chats and giggling our way late into the evening, until it was time to catch up with other guys for a quick snack before heading back to study sessions late into the night. And then again, mounted on his Yamaha bike, we would roam about during midnights in the city lights.

After a hiatus, his priorities took him to Mumbai where he made giant strides in his career later. We lost touch until after few years, when he got in touch again; he wanted me to be there too, make a career & life. He had morally supported me big way, guiding me through all the tribulations like a mentor and made sure that he was always there for me. He felt happy to be getting married, though the marriage later fell apart and indirectly proved to be his nemesis for their long courtship.

He would pick me up from the lows after I failed at making it through in the interviews. At times strangely enough, he rued' that he was not doing enough for me. Perhaps he felt he was not giving enough time for me, so he convinced me to stay with his family, brushing aside my concerns of intruding into their newly married life. He acted big brother at times. After staying with them for few months, I moved to a separate apartment, since having settled in my job, I was getting married too. Cannot forget the moments of lazy Sunday afternoons spent in mindless banters, leg-pulling, or those of him dragging me to the gym.

On getting married, on a lighter side, I introduced him to my in-laws as my friend, my bro, my psychiatrist, my mechanic, and boss, all rolled into one. After a few years, we lost touch again. For some years he was in oblivion, though I was in the know that he fell into rough patch after a failed marriage and got lost in another world. Life seems so predictable and yet it is not. The life's terrains saw us taking several unplanned detours, merging again, but then falling apart after going a distance.

Then it was one eventful day. I did not hear from him for long, the last thing I heard of him is getting admitted for some ailment. That day, amidst the joys of shifting to our new home the next day, I got the news that he had succumbed to Liver Cirhossis that he fought so hard. I could only rue that I could not be at his side to share a few moments, cheer him up and now what remains of him are memories of the last call from the hospital I had with him, prodding me to "like" his songs and posts on the social media.

Recollecting myself to face the work day, I glanced at the sky as if seeking answers from the heavens. He was no more, but still, in the life's many decisions, I still used to consult him & do as it would have appeared right to him. Overwhelmed, as if hallucinating things, it seemed like he stepped into my room, and say what he often did- quote that iconic dialogue from the Hindi movie "Anand": "Come, let us go for a ride, you lazy bum! *Mahesh Babu- Zindagi lambi nahi, badi honi chahiye!*" (Life should be bigger, and not longer!) and he dragged me out again.

XVII

A magical, musical journey

The world music day is observed on 21-June, to honour the musicians and singers. The artists, through the ages, have had us entertained through their varied creations. Today music is an integral part of our lives, a proven stress buster for its' meditative effects. But as much as the day is about the artists and the musical instruments, the history of the medium is also as long and interesting.

There are many music apps today that stream music on-demand and a true connoisseur doesn't have any space, genre, time or location restraints to enjoy pure, unfiltered joys of music. While the current generation may not have much inkling, the medium has its own big story of evolution, emotional strings attached! Well, *baat niklegi to phir door talak jayegi!!*

Now, prior to the era preceding our generation- "Gen-X" (i.e, the 80s) and before, the Indian music scene was little quirky, since it was the privilege of a select few, having a refined taste. At a time that majority of us were still trapped under the conservative mindset, making even music a taboo subject! There were not many choices in terms of singers or genres either.

It was the era of the Gramophone- though we practically never witnessed one, except in old Hindi films (*Chashme Baddoor*, for instance). But, like it was about the advent of television - people in the neighbourhood used to huddle under that one roof where they had a TV set (remember the catchy phrase "neighbour's envy, owners' pride"?)- it was similarly a status symbol to own one!

It didn't matter what music the owner host played, but mostly it used to be some classical music! Placing the reader pin gently over a rotating, large disc with diameter comparable to Adnan Sami's waistline (when he entered the music scene) and slowly, the music would play out- which was way slower too, so you can as well imagine the black-n-white hero taking all the time in the world for the "*aalaap*" before coming to the point- his girlfriend having dumped him for some better-off clerk working in the local post office.

For the generation that grew up during the 60's and 70's, the transistor Radios have been to them- what smart phones have been to us. Popular among the masses, they brought respite to the construction labourers. The folklore and media popularized the idea of people, wanting to get latest bytes of cricket or music- glued to their radio sets at certain hours of the day; extrapolated to all day along, if you happened to be a *babu* (clerk) in some govt department, provided your "*sahab*" (boss) is not looking at you.

The soldiers (or F*aujis*' as they used to be fondly called), similarly at remote, distant postings, with no other means of entertainment, used to think of their family back home, and *farmaish* some film song on the *Jaimaala* program and the host would, on his request, call out names of his kith and kin on his behalf, sending ripples of joys on hearing the family man's voice, to those tuned in back home. Music thus, formed a deeper connect. Thanks to the radios, the magical, personal touch used to get conveyed to the soldiers' family living in a distant place!

Then there were bigger, immobile versions too, around which you could imagine many people from the neighbourhood, grippingly waiting on the bytes from the Indo-Pak war. You could as well be excused for the opinion, that given a potent payload, these huge radio sets could have doubled up as lethal bombs themselves!

Then came along tapes (Audio cassettes), which hold the lion's share of our nostalgia. Though long past their shelf lives, in many a home, they are still kept adorning the shelves as ornamental pieces.

Now, for the interesting part- due to frequent footfalls, the *Paan* shops (Paan is an edible preparation taken after meals for better digestion) in the neighbourhood doubled up as music stores. So, all day long, they would belt out latest Hindi movie songs of the times (90s)- which used to be music for us, but noise for the elderly, hence were received with a look of disgust. That explains why, any new addition bought excitingly from a faraway shop and being tested at full volume, earned us the epithet of a "*paanthela wala*" from the elders. For them, it was a "trial by music" no less!

For the major part, the audio cassettes would find their way home if parents were generous enough with pocket money. Or you would have to cut the corners if you were the oppressed lot. The cassette in question would either be an album, or a combo of films (A/B sides) or a customized selection of songs to be recorded from some audio cassette store. One aficionado had a whole cassette recorded with just one song all over- both the sides, so he doesn't have to do the rewind/forward business! So, it mattered least knowing which "side" was being played at any moment, but mattered more- that the song narrates the protagonist's love reduced to being "one-sided" too!! I will leave readers with the exercise of guessing the Attaullah Khan song.

At times, the "rewinder" or the "forward" or both would not work. Such times, you hold the cassette over the tip of a ball pen, and move it in rotary motion, akin to operating Lord Krishna's "*Sudarshan chakra*". Until the start or end of the either side is reached, ready to be played all over again.

Sometimes, the price consideration would cause us oppressed lot to use a blank cassette or if there none's at our disposal (being the super-oppressed lot, again), re-use the "least favourite/used/noticed" audio cassette from your collection, to be overwritten using the "desired one" borrowed from someone, and tape recorded at home. The side effects of this DIY exercise were that such a session also caught the surrounding sounds-thumps thuds, and the hushed voices interspersed; the end result was understood to be of inferior quality.

Now, the audio cassettes were untrustworthy beasts, for one. In between a song, the old cassettes would play spoilsport, and start hissing. So, you know it got messed up inside – and wasting no time, you eject the fighter pilot in grave danger inside. And attempt to intricately salvage the stuck cassette reel around the magnetic reader. Sometimes it would break, causing us to do damage control- a series of cut-n-paste ops with a cello tape or nail polish- lest the big bro should find out about the step-brotherly treatment meted to his fav audio cassette. But find out, anyways he would, once he notices a few words missing in the second "*mukhadaa*"- so, it is time for you to face the music; building a case for your "*dukhadaa*"!

Waiting in the wings, the Walkman came next. It was actually first personal music system, to talk about, actually. Though cassettes were still an evil necessity, powered by battery, it was cool to carry along music everywhere.

And then came the era of MP3 players- which allowed us to store hundreds of audio files in a tiny device and also wield the power to play any random song at will. It is still nostalgic to think of the US trip when eventfully I laid hands on one; and being amused at the new ways it allowed us to operate it. The untrustworthy tapes would soon be relegated to history!

The MP3 players were short lived, though, since many big-ticket revolutions were waiting in the anvil- the media's carrying capacities were increasing day by day and the smartphones allowed the fusion of many different things - music included, into a smartly rolled package.

And so- it took a visit to my home where it all begun. At one corner of my room were lying all those memories- the radio set, the tape recorder and the cassettes, the MP3 player, iPod touch, etc. They may be obsolete- they cannot talk any longer, but, like an old flame they do talk of the times! And, like the hypnotic spell of Miyaan Tansen or the Pied Piper from Hamlin, given a closer look- they hold the power, to mesmerize you, and urge you to take a walk down the memory lane! Well, as the Hindi song goes, *"Karoge Yaad to Har Baat Yaad Aayegi"*...

XVIII

That eventful day...

...life was bustling with activity, since I was engaged a fortnight back and we were destined to get married by the year end. I returned to Mumbai, so caught up with pleasant, heart-warming thoughts of the months preceding the marriage. Though I was unaware of the impending peril that awaited me; no warnings either, barring one that is often laughed off about, talking of marriages. Well, it was certainly not about "weathering" the storms in marriage, for it was really, a very bad rainy day- Mumbai was submerged on that fateful day. The calendar that day, read: 26-July, 2005.

It was a re-run of the cry-wolf story actually. People had long stopped paying attention to the weather bureau advisories already. Politicians are to promises what weathermen are to their forecasts- not to be taken seriously. They issued a warning of very heavy rain that day too, which everyone turned a deaf ear to. People carried their BAU (Business-As-Usual) and so did many organizations, my company included. Owing to late breakfast, I ate very little that noon, so around snacks time I checked with our cafeteria for options on the menu. Only to know that the vendor did not turn up due to rains. So, I joined a few colleagues tuned in to the news bytes on a big TV in the cafeteria.

The weather bytes had grown a lot in intensity compared to that a few hours back. Until an hour back the news was about public transport going kaput; so those relying on personal vehicles were not concerned at all. The mobile networks were jammed already. It was imperative that like every monsoon, people, groups and companies would bow down before the undoing of our great municipal corporation; and that the employees would soon be allowed to rush back to their homes, so basically all were chilled out but taking care not to express ecstasy writ on their faces in front of their bosses.

But now it was different. Soon our company realized that the weather guys were really serious about what they said. And so, too little too late- it announced on its public address system so that people can take an informed decision; and stay back in case there is nothing better to look up to for the travel back home (e.g., Helicopter, *Superman* on the standby, etc).

Being optimistic that nothing would happen to us & we can still make it on our own, some of us started out. The realization came late, about a KM from office, that it was no time for such foolishness. My bike gave in, refusing to start again- and with no help in vicinity, the thought of pulling on through another 26 KMS was terrifying! Hence, seeing no other option, like a few others, I abandoned my bike aside to join two other office mates. And like everyone in the sea of humanity around, we continued rest of the journey on foot- wading through the strong, waist-deep waters.

As popularized by the images of that fateful day on the public domain, people made human chains holding each other's hands, trusting their lives with complete strangers. There were horrors witnessed too, like that instance, when one of a few adventurous guys was apparently not following this simple hand-holding safety protocol. He failed to anticipate the manhole camouflaged under the strong current. Before our eyes, he got overpowered and swept away by the flow, leading him straight to an imminent end inside a manhole.

We walked a few kilometres, looking for some road side stall and we did find one, albeit a very crowded one. I luckily managed to grab a *vada-pav*, my last known meal for next 3 days. We anyways, continued marching.

The traffic moved at snails' pace, so we tried asking for lift along the way, which did not work unfortunately. Eventually we tried something else - I was lucky enough to manage to run, hop & latch on to a truck while the others were not. That was relief since 5 KMS were written off from my tiresome homebound journey. It was an experience hanging on to back of the truck with space barely enough to stand.

When it took a detour at some point, I jumped off and continued on foot again. The scene was similar for the rest of the route. Electricity was shut off for next few days, so were the petrol pumps and ATMs. All the vehicles plying were perhaps making their last trip before things were restored to normalcy. The autorickshaw drivers were quoting outrageous fares, so I rather decided to walk the last 5 kms too. I reached home safely to discover deep rashes developed since I wore jeans to the office that day. My basic mobile refused to cater to my basic need- I could not communicate on my safety to my parents staying in another city. The sore feet ensured that hunger did not matter and soon I was in deep slumber.

For the next few "darker" days, nearby grocery stores were shut, since supplies were affected. Hunger was felt in between, but things got little better, when on 3rd day our building residents pooled in to arrange something for dinner on the terrace flat. More than hunger, though, it was a constant thought worrying about the parents back home & others waiting to hear a word from me. Mobile networks took good enough time to be restored. Nature was at its furious best- the water levels were not relenting. The mind was constantly hooked on to any story that came our way of people getting stuck somewhere in the deluge.

After 3 days, water levels receded and things looked up. Services - electricity, petrol pumps, ATMs, transport, supplies, eateries, mobile networks, etc slowly started getting restored. After getting my mis-behaving phone repaired & assuring people back home, I visited the very place to find my bike parked aside now with lots of trash from flood sticking to it from all the sides. After that getting repaired, my life got back on track.

All the talks of periodic emergency response drills now made so much sense to people (Or so I guess). On another extremes, the higher-ups back then used to brush off their administrative inefficiencies under the carpet, lauding the spirit of resilient city dwellers'- whereas in reality, the entire island city was in standstill and people had no choice but to walk long distances, and do such things as a matter of survival. Now, when I look back on the timeline, it is hard to believe such a thing ever happened. We are astonished equally when we see that many people and organizations still fail to learn the lessons & do the needful, hence, as they say, the history is damned to repeat itself.

XIX

The Malaise within

A malaise, if allowed to fester over longer time, may potentially turn carcinogenic, so it is a better idea to take a pause, reflect and apply corrective measures- regardless of the painful memories that the process may bring. Even though bitter, a medicine aids in better recovery and coupled with preventive steps, holds promise for long standing benefits. That holds true, be it any matter concerning personal/public health or any prevailing issue of governance.

The other day, while on a cleaning spree over the weekend, my wife & myself chanced upon what looked like some muddy structure, just over the shelf where the unused bed linens were kept, and extending up to the adjacent wall. Taking a closer look, and next moment we were in for a shock at the sight of what seemed like some live termites. The cleaning discontinued. In order to confirm, we called our maid. She seconded our opinion informing us of the urgency of tackling it on priority, lest all the furniture would soon be eaten away if allowed to spread any further.

Caught unawares, that put everything out of order- the orderliness of things, the day's schedule, and, that for the coming few days as well! As per leads from the housing society office, it was time for the pest control contract to kick in. But not so soon, since it would take at least a fortnight, as they were unable to fetch our contract records with a third-party vendor. Reason being that the vendor office was facing the issue of termites themselves, and pest-control and sanitization of customer records were underway at their end! Hence, until we heard from them, we had to make do with their spot fixing, a workaround for the time being! Till such time, things needed a thorough check for sanitization, before being kept at a safe distance away from the walls, to cut short the spread.

Our lives were thrown out of gear; we were agonized for days to come- until vendor confirmed on deep, affirmative pest treatment that would ensure our imminent sanity.

This termite issue was one of the examples of how life takes 180 degrees turn- we had to keep everything deemed important till that point aside and deal with the problem in hand. The challenge was to keep our sanity intact in the midst of the mess, while carrying out the regular, mundane tasks and face the routine challenges as well.

On my part, I had joined another company around a year back, and was still getting to know things. Hence it was imperative to put in more hours to get a good grip at the project. Things were, though, still laid back on the work front, hence while working from home, I took the liberty to finish off other personal tasks, including devoting certain hours for a few days checking every nook & corner for any other visible indications.

Now, googling on the termites threw a few startling facts about them! A housing complex like ours was susceptible since it is close to a creek. Now, it starts with the king, who gives lifelong company to the queen, who, in turn makes for an interesting mothers' day story! The couple go underground to turn over a new leaf. The life-long job of a queen termite is to produce millions and millions of worker and soldier termites! The queen & the king lay several feet deep inside the ground where the queen can start reproducing and lay eggs every 3 seconds. That is, until the queen cannot reproduce any longer, so the workers lick her to death. The workers move up and down all day and night, scrambling for food and making several vaulted chambers and tunnels along the vertical pathways of the damp building walls. That is how they make inroads even in very high rises. Such a colony can be loosely called, as such, a company raised using "bottom-up" approach!

The interesting trivia aside, after a while, the long wait was getting on my nerves, both for the pest problem at hand and on the work front. For the latter part, the nature of work had me in a fix, I was disillusioned from the start, though I was not sure what it was which left me feeling uncomfortable. Maybe it was some aspect of new work culture or some inconvenient truth for which I needed to brace up; whatever, but I was struggling to make it work. It dawned upon me quite late, just like the revelation of termites. At the outset, most of my time went working on the non-core areas. I was losing the motivation very fast. That, despite my clarity w.r.t my objectives to the HR before being on-boarded.

Coming to the middle & lower levels management, whatever the work-culture (or lack of it), that usually gets driven "top-down", it boiled down to absence of any sustainable, healthy practice, paying the least regards to the employee aspirations. The laid-back attitude could be seen in general amongst the middle-level "administrative" managers who had no inkling what it took to develop innovative solutions. The feedback loop was conspicuous by its absence; hence rigidity was the norm. Very soon, with absence of any support, I slowly started drifting away, losing the required steam.

Then, in the meanwhile, there was this revelation of a big scandal doing media rounds, involving our parent company. Every decision of the CEO's scandalous tenure came under scanner. And as much as their PR scrambled into action for the face-saving cover-ups whilst investigation was underway, back home, the unsettling thought of termites constantly haunted us, driving us paranoid.

I got tired of putting up with the obnoxious, unprofessional behavior but lived up with that disillusionment for quite some time. Like what the termites did to the wooden shelf, something was eating me within. Termites were everywhere, in the world outside, as well as the world inside me.

The pest control guys figured out things, and turned up finally, and after a day more of discomfort and inconvenience, the issue was finally resolved to our satisfaction. When they started, I noticed an insect coming out from the small crevice in the wall. Seems it was not a termite- it either did not belong or did not want to! I took the hint and moved on.

XX
Indian Parking League

After the isolating effects of pandemic, if there is anything that stops us on our tracks, and prevents us from heading out, it is the traffic jam. It seems like people, who held their horses for too long waiting for the pandemic to end, begun pouring out on streets and highways- as if there is no tomorrow. As if road-rage was not enough an issue to deal with, mankind now also had to deal with "revenge" travel. Talking especially of cities like Mumbai that are already bursting at the seams, the Google Maps shows almost all the roads leading to the city & outside in red, reducing many areas fit enough to be metaphorically called red-light areas. The red colour is indicative of the blood boiling for people stuck for hours at such traffic jams, raging to explode on the road.

When jams happen at such a massive scale as we witnessed over the last few months, the designated parking lots lose their meaning due to hard to resolve deadlocks. People can neither park, hence stuck at entrances, for the lots are filled to the capacity; nor can they drive off from these lots, since exits are blocked for the same reason- roads outside are filled to the capacity! With literally no movement, the vehicles appear, as parked, sometimes for hours altogether. The world seems an extension of the parking lots. Such traffic woes led the learned sages meditating at the Himalayas to exclaim, thus: *Vasudhaiva Parking-Sthala Asti*- the whole world is a parking lot.

The frequency of such massive traffic jams shows no signs of abating for few big reasons. The incorrectly parked vehicles at the sides also leave very little room of whatever is left of the rain-filled, pothole decorated roads. Coupled with the many infrastructure projects aimed at transforming Mumbai into another Shanghai, the municipal guys proactively dig up roads all through the year, thereby helping traffic police in bringing traffic to a complete standstill.

As a result, quite often, sitting at home, I look out from my window & ponder over the best way to take to go to point B. Sensing a similar situation, a great 19th century poet, sitting in his balcony similar to mine, once remarked- "Life is tough. All roads lead to nowhere". Now I know, why they call it "home sweet home".

Though venture out, you may- depending on how much of adventure is left in you. Just like the other day that we did – visiting a mall for a movie- my kid, my wife and her worst half. But hardly a KM away, we were caught in a thick traffic jam already; it was not going anywhere. Ironically, sometime back I was concerned so much about finding a parking space at the mall!

In many such instances of longer traffic jams, many tea and peanut vendors believing in "time is money" also sprout up, making the wait less painful. Once the wait lasted 3.5 hours, which is big enough time to actually step out, go watch a movie, and come back! I think at this rate, the day is not far, when the best way to drive from point A to point B, would be to get out of the car, leave it as is parked on the road, and start walking instead.

Anyways, now only a few minutes were remaining for catching up with the movie and here, we were, watching each other's faces instead of the movie, munching peanuts instead of popcorn. Us & the others outside were bounded by a common emotion- anger.

At the next traffic island, we were stopped again by the symbolic red signal, as if they needed one to stop us! By now bored of staring at each other, we looked outside. Around us were many bikers waiting eagerly to charge ahead at the earliest sign of green. I was reminded of Changez (or "Genghis") Khan & Co. Same aggression, like the racists at the race-course (also called horsemen), mounted atop horses; ready to take on a sprinting start, only restricted by the sight of traffic police providing a stiff resistance on traffic island across the Sindhu River.

Talking of the fearsome Mongols- whom Genghis Khan (a big racist himself) led, they make for interesting historical characters. Known for their characteristic agility & speed, there was a big reason behind their successes - they never stopped in their voyages (unlike us dutiful citizens who respect traffic cops where present) undertaken for conquering other territories; not even for taking *tea/cigarette* breaks. So adept were they with their horses, that they never wasted their time even for the purposes of sleep- they caught winks riding on the horses, saving them time on the longer sojourns in a big way; and mind it- that meant no *tea/cigarette* breaks for the horses either!

Mongols were the least fun-loving people that time, I guess. It is debatable whether they allowed the troops Sundays off for catching up with latest movie, popcorn included. But, I think, in all possibilities, they did not. Well, two good reasons for that. One- Sunday or Monday- all the time, they were too passionate about invading other territories, so much so as to exclude from the mix anything like a movie for temporary entertainment. Two- popcorn was not invented back then.

Now, as we know from the humankind's experience- all thanks to the divine popcorn, our civilization not only survived multiple assaults from guys like Genghis, but we also made it through landmark movies like *Roy*, *Saanwariya* and *Dhaakad*, all thanks to pop-corn tubs (which can double up as vessels such times to store water from the tears). I am sure, Genghis would have liked the idea of being treated to *The Thugs of Hindostan*, with popcorn for the sides.

Popcorn or not, as we are told by the historians, food was a major issue they faced everywhere- and the reason is simple- they killed all hotel guys too, without entertaining the thoughts of dinner. So, when they ran out of food, they simply used to cook a few horses for dinner. We can empathise at some level with Genghis & Co for this, though. That is because, like they did for the horses, we feel similarly for the popcorn guy - when, coming straight from the horse's mouth, we are told that the popcorn is finished!

"Charge ahead, *Yalgaar*!!!" – I was bolted out of my thoughts by the sight of the fellow racist Genghis Khans' jumping on their horns and spitting out some unprintable $^%*&#. The signal had eventfully changed to green, ushering in the merrymaking era of movie plus popcorn awaiting us at the finishing line. Somehow, we made it through and reached the mall's parking lot. Cars seen here there, everywhere but not a place to park ours! And that's where our differences end with Genghis Khan! Am sure if he were born in this age, he would similarly be caught up in fix on where to park his horses.

"We've only 2 parking slots now"

"Oh, but we need 3".

"Sorry *bro*, can't help it. *Baahar lagaa lo kahin*. (Park it elsewhere outside the mall) "

And you know very well what that means- exposing the horses to the watchful eyes of the traffic police waiting in the towing vehicle at a distance. Conversely, Genghis bro would have figured the way out as well- let's cook the third horse.

Driven by the desire for a good time, we wished the parking ordeal to end soon. Mostly I will show up few more minutes late into the movie; so, letting the duo accompanying me to carry on- myself, the third horse, galloped ahead, hopeful of finding a parking slot nearby. *Yalgaar*!

Desi Soup - Err - Men:
(A Compilation) Kindle Edition

by Mahesh Balasubramanian (Author)   Format: Kindle Edition

ಐ

Top Reviews:

"It is a good read. Your style of writing and playing with the pun is refreshing. May you write and publish many more books."
- **Mrs. Kaumudi Patil**

ಹಿ

Mahesh debuts with an engaging anthology of nine articles. He plucks colourful threads from everyday life and weaves a tapestry of experiences, anecdotes and reflections. The short, crisp articles are relatable and laced with his unique sense of humour.
Mahesh is no doubt a compelling narrator. The write-ups keep the reader engaged and at the same time coerce him to introspect– and wait for more!"
- **Mrs. Rekha Narsikar**

ಹಿ

Mahesh Balasubramanian has a very unique way of expressing his observations- decorating them with his sense of humour, a bit of suspense, lot of thrill! They carry high standard of language. The writeups are very crisp & well researched, with not a moment of lull, thereby keeping readers hooked."
- **Mrs. Sandhya Deshpande**

ಹಿ

Satire at its best, the book is a must read- excellent writing skills and Mahesh plays with words so wisely. Very balanced...every article is relevant. Excellent debut...waiting for many more; hopefully in a different genre.."
- **Mr. Nandkumar Iyer**

ৎ

Amazing book, esp for those who love reading humour and keeps things simple.

It keeps smile on your face while reading each chapter and you connect so easily. A must read especially who loves humour and keep things simple. The writer, Mr. Mahesh plays with words so effortlessly and effectively. I recommend everyone to go and read "Desi soup" Sweet and Spicy!!"

- **Mr. Dinkar Iyer**

ৎ

Desi Soup-Err-Men (E-Book)is available on Amazon Kindle, priced at (INR) Rs.49/-.

About The Author

Mahesh Balasubramanian is a software professional based in Mumbai. His articles are a regular feature in the leading national newspaper from Nagpur, "The Hitavada". He discovered his funny side when his boss called him "funny" on getting "ages" in response to a query asking the timeline for a task.

When he's not working, he pretends to be working hard – a carefully crafted formula which has so far worked to his favour and seen him through the 16 years in software profession. Despite being very buzy doing nothing, he still finds time to write on all and sundry.

When not doing anything above, he loves to travel, observe people, read and play mindgames like chess, sudoku and irritate the people around.

9 798888 338827